BOOK ONE

Beautiful

Artistic Music that Promotes
Technical Development at the Piano

Selected and Edited by **Victoria McArthur**

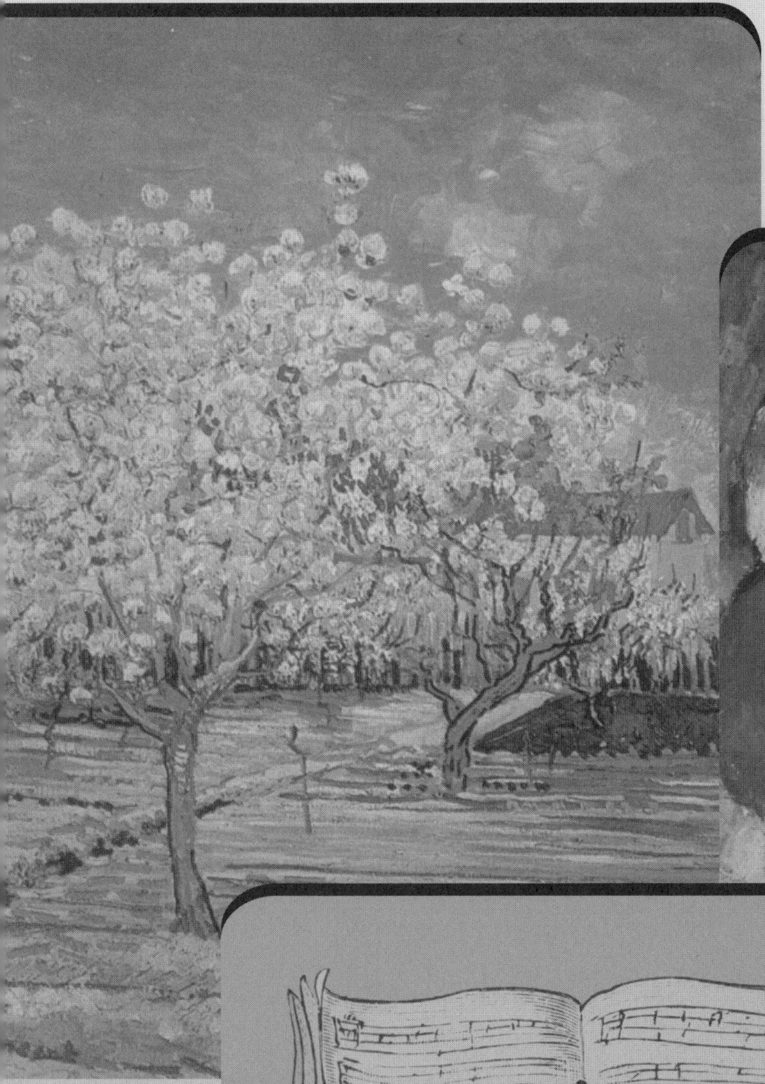

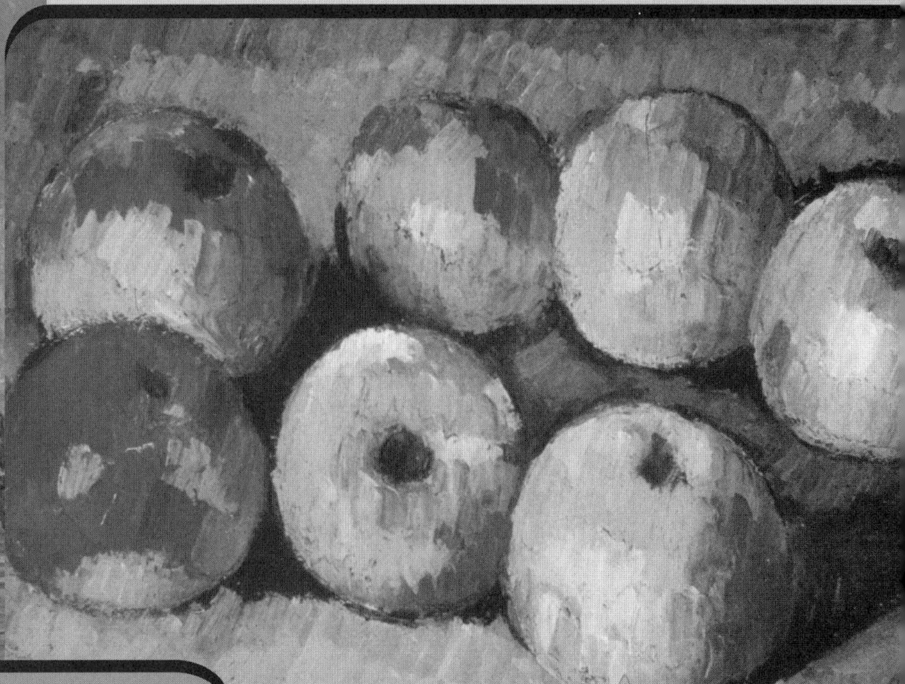

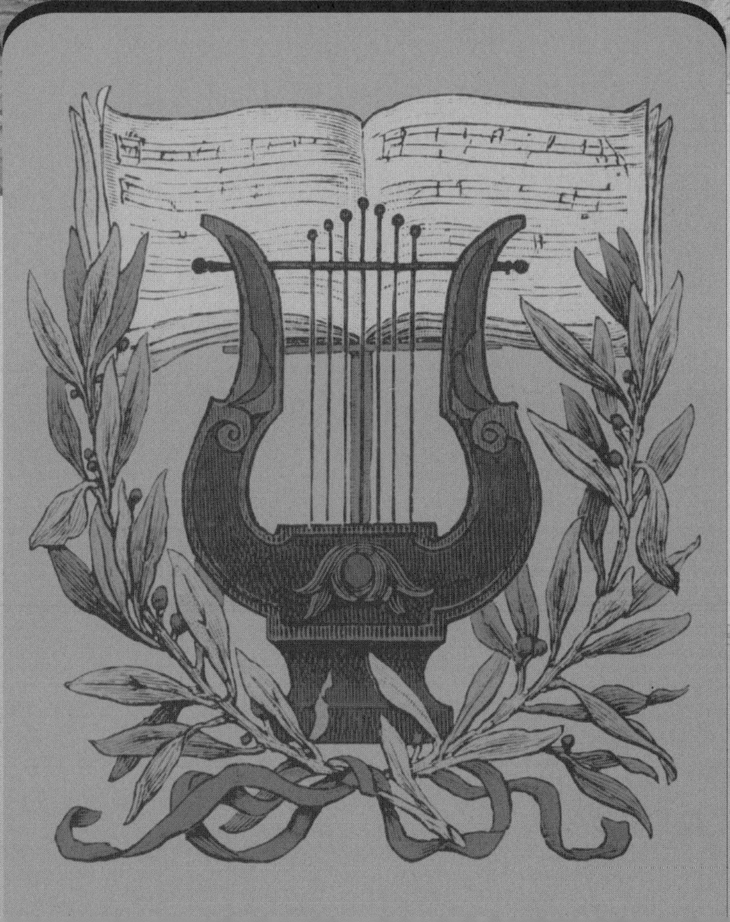

ISBN 0-7390-1944-9

Alfred

Foreword

TO TEACHERS

Etudes have provided pianists with valuable technical training for generations. Today's pianists have more demands on their time than ever before, therefore, the materials chosen for study should be of the highest musical quality, worthy of the time expenditure. The pieces in *Beautiful Etudes* have been tested and chosen by piano students and teachers not only for their technical effectiveness but also because they are lovely musical works.

UNIQUE FEATURES

- 16 artistic piano studies in five-finger patterns
- Arranged in progressive order of difficulty
- Renotated in bass and treble clef, when needed, for reading ease
- Sharps or flats appear as accidentals (instead of key signatures)
- Position changes highlighted
- Difficult rhythms clarified
- Alternate fingering suggestions for small hands

OTHER FEATURES

- Technical goals for each etude
- Composer biographical information
- Practice directions for each etude
- Suggested keys for transposition
- Creative suggestions for further musical and technical exploration
- Teacher/parent duet parts for selected etudes
- Mastery and memorization checklists
- Glossary

SUGGESTIONS FOR TEACHERS

- Play each etude for the student. Modeling of expressive playing is essential to convey musical and technical ideals.
- Provide concrete practice steps for the student, including slow, hands separate practice with a metronome.

Table of Contents

NOTE: Most titles are editorial.

BEFORE YOU PLAY

On the closed key cover, "play" hands together as you count aloud.

AS YOU PLAY

- Notice that both hands play one octave higher than written.
- Listen carefully so both hands play exactly together.
- Practice both hands at the same dynamic level.

TRANSPOSE

- *Stepping Stones* is written in C major.
- Transpose to G major.
- Now transpose to F major. Which note is flat?______

CREATE

- Play the RH louder than the LH.
- Play the LH louder than the RH.

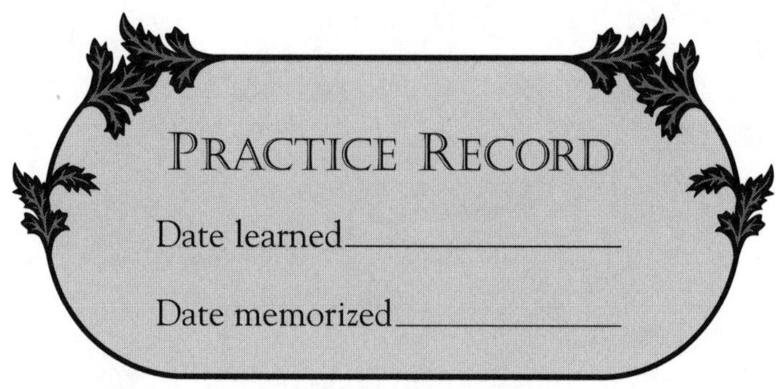

Ferdinand Beyer (1803–1863), German, was best known for his arrangements of music originally written for orchestra and opera. He wrote a comprehensive piano method that is still used by teachers today.

Stepping Stones

Op. 101, No. 7

Ferdinand Beyer

Moderato

Both hands one octave higher than written throughout

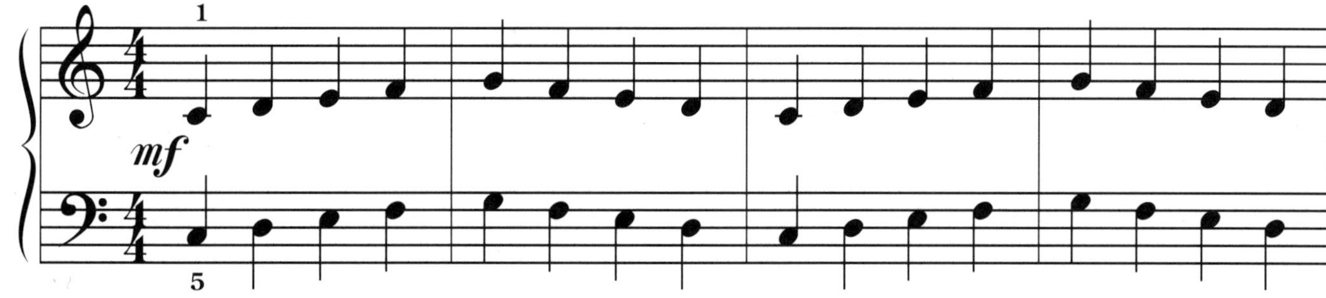

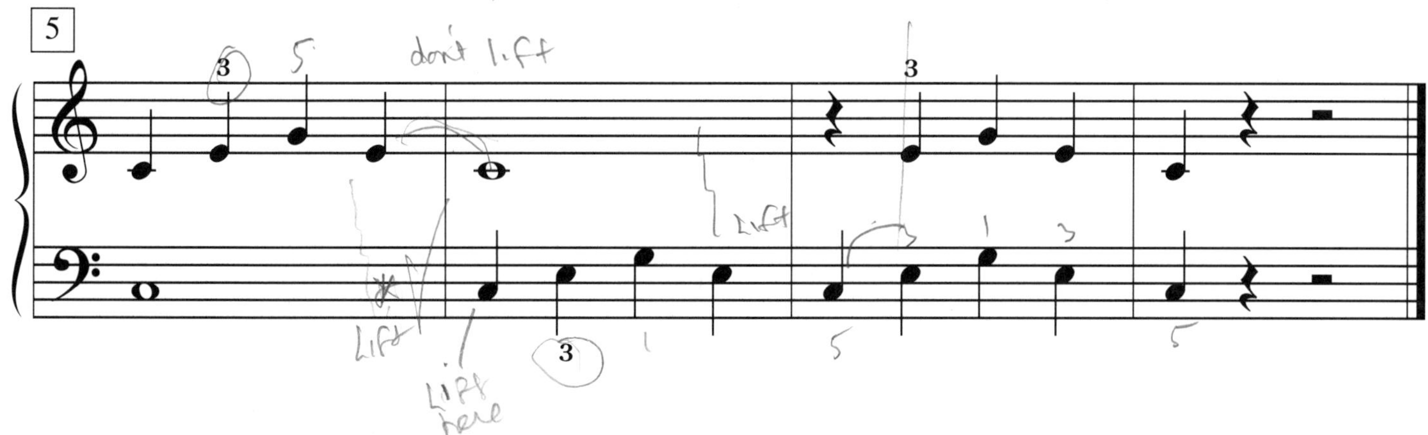

Teacher or Parent

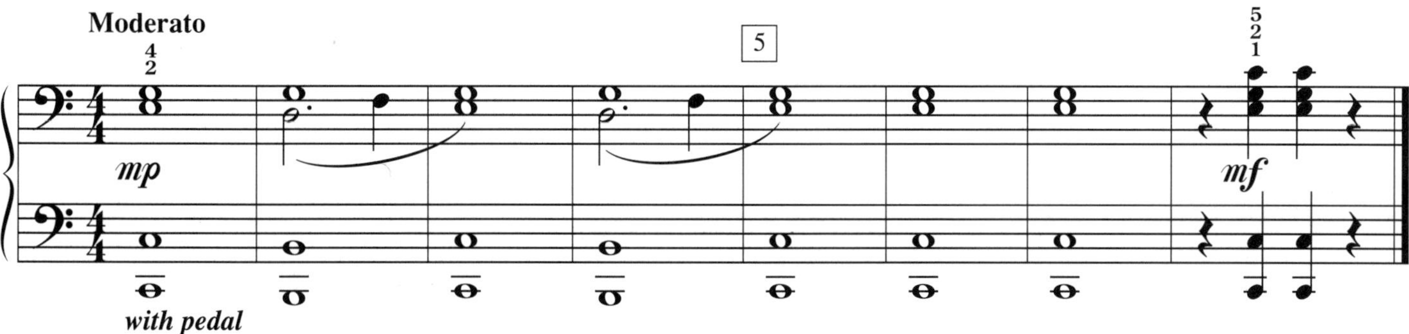

BEFORE YOU PLAY

- This piece uses mostly steps (2nds). Circle all the skips (3rds).
- On the closed key cover, "play" each hand separately, then together.

AS YOU PLAY

- Listen and decide which hand has the melody. Play that part louder.
- Play both hands exactly together in measures 1–7 and measures 13–15.

TRANSPOSE

- *Ode to Joy* is written in C major. The starting note for both hands is E, the third note in C major.
- Transpose to G major. What is the starting note for both hands?_______

CREATE

- Vary *Ode to Joy* by choosing your own dynamics. Make the most joyful part the loudest.

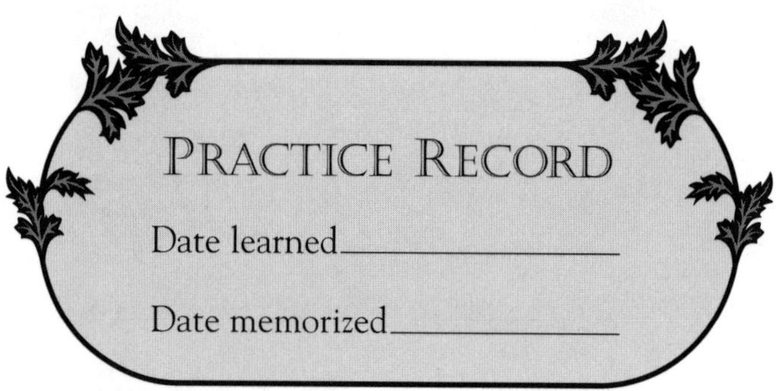

Ludwig van Beethoven (1770–1827), German, is one of the best known of all classical composers. The *Ode to Joy* theme from his Ninth Symphony is loved and recognized by people throughout the world.

Ode to Joy

Ludwig van Beethoven
Arr. Victoria McArthur

Allegretto

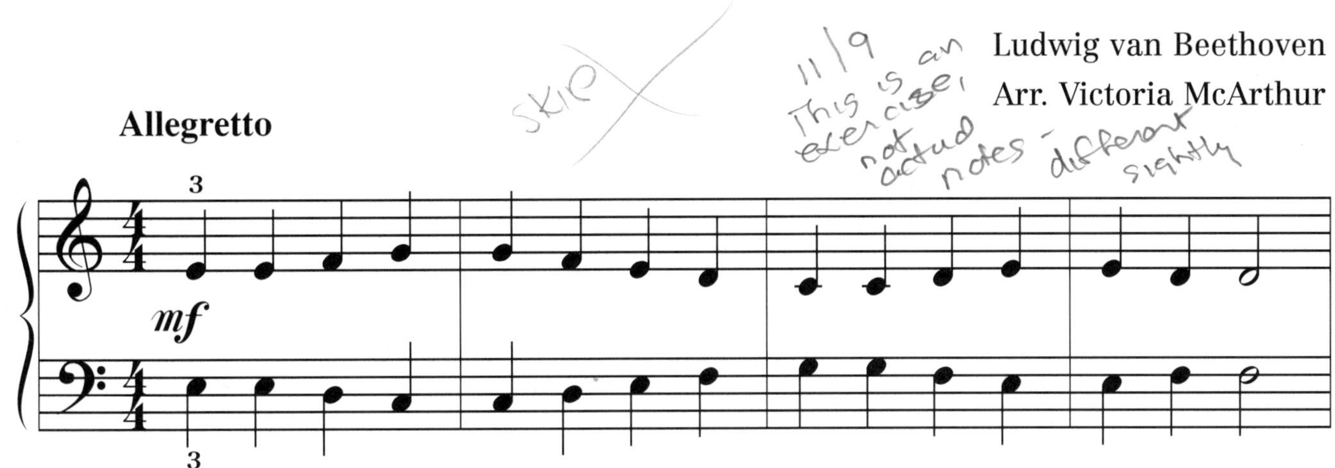

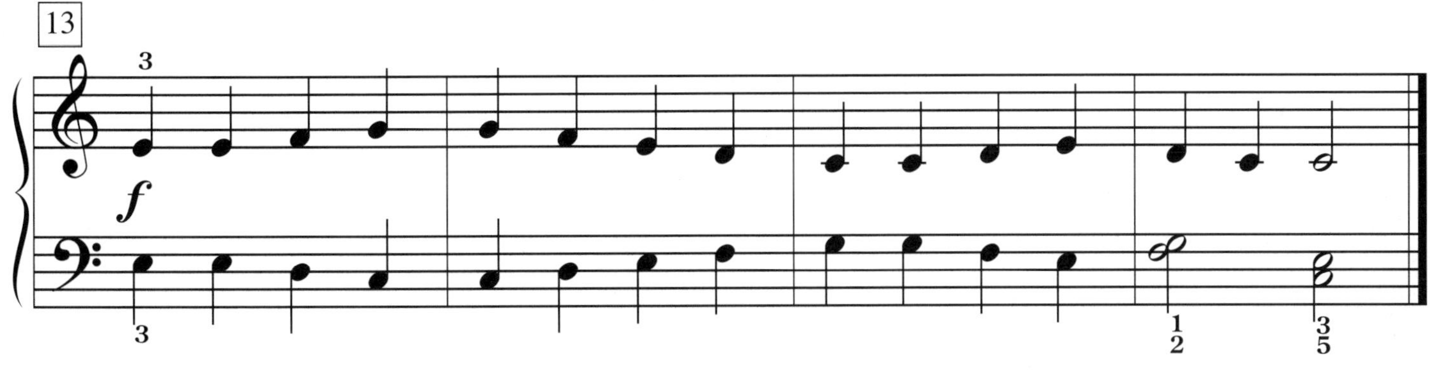

BEFORE YOU PLAY

- Tap the rhythm hands together on your lap, counting aloud.
- On the closed key cover, "play" hands together.

AS YOU PLAY

- Notice that both hands play one octave higher than written.
- Listen to decide which hand has the melody. Play that part louder.
- Be careful that the notes for both hands sound at exactly the same time.

TRANSPOSE

- *Singing Voices* is written in C major. The LH starts on E, the third note in C major.
- Transpose to D major. What is the starting LH note in D major?_______♯

CREATE

- Play *Singing Voices* staccato. Does this version sound good with the teacher part? Why or why not?

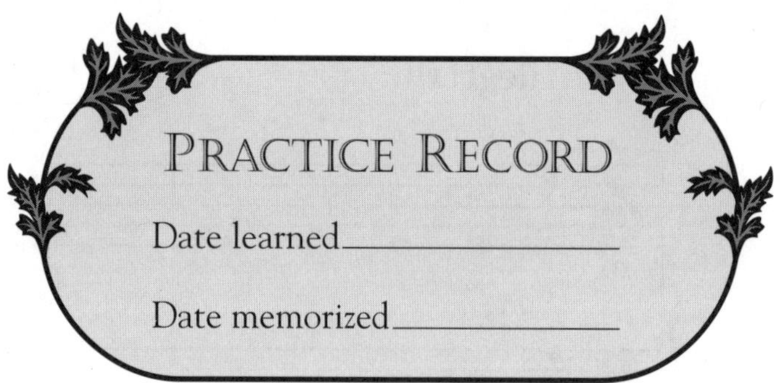

Ferdinand Beyer (1803–1863), *see page 4.*

Teacher or Parent

Singing Voices

Op. 101, No. 11

No skips on the qtr notes - only

11/9/05
11/16/05
12/7/05
1/11/06
1/18
1/25

Ferdinand Beyer

Moderato

Both hands one octave higher than written throughout

Parallel motion
Next note up or down

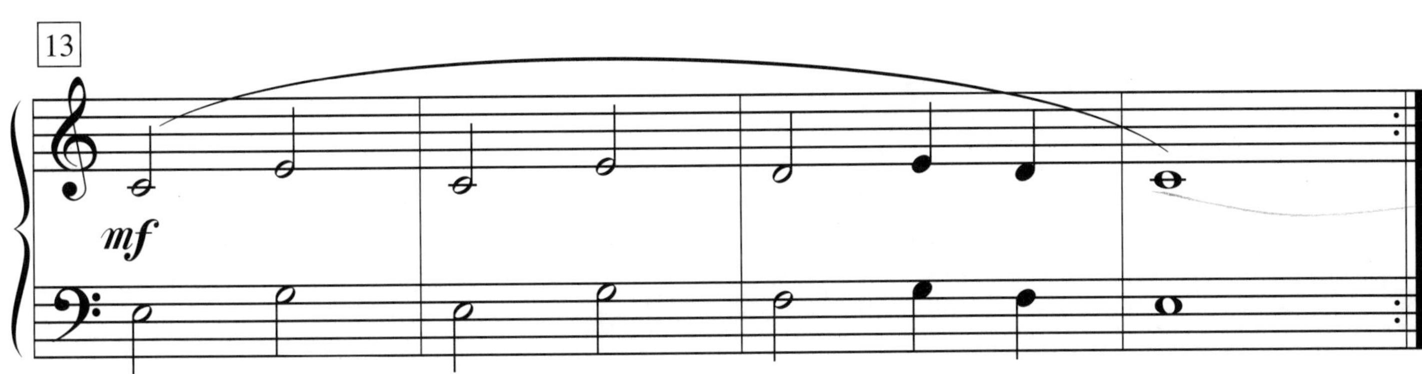

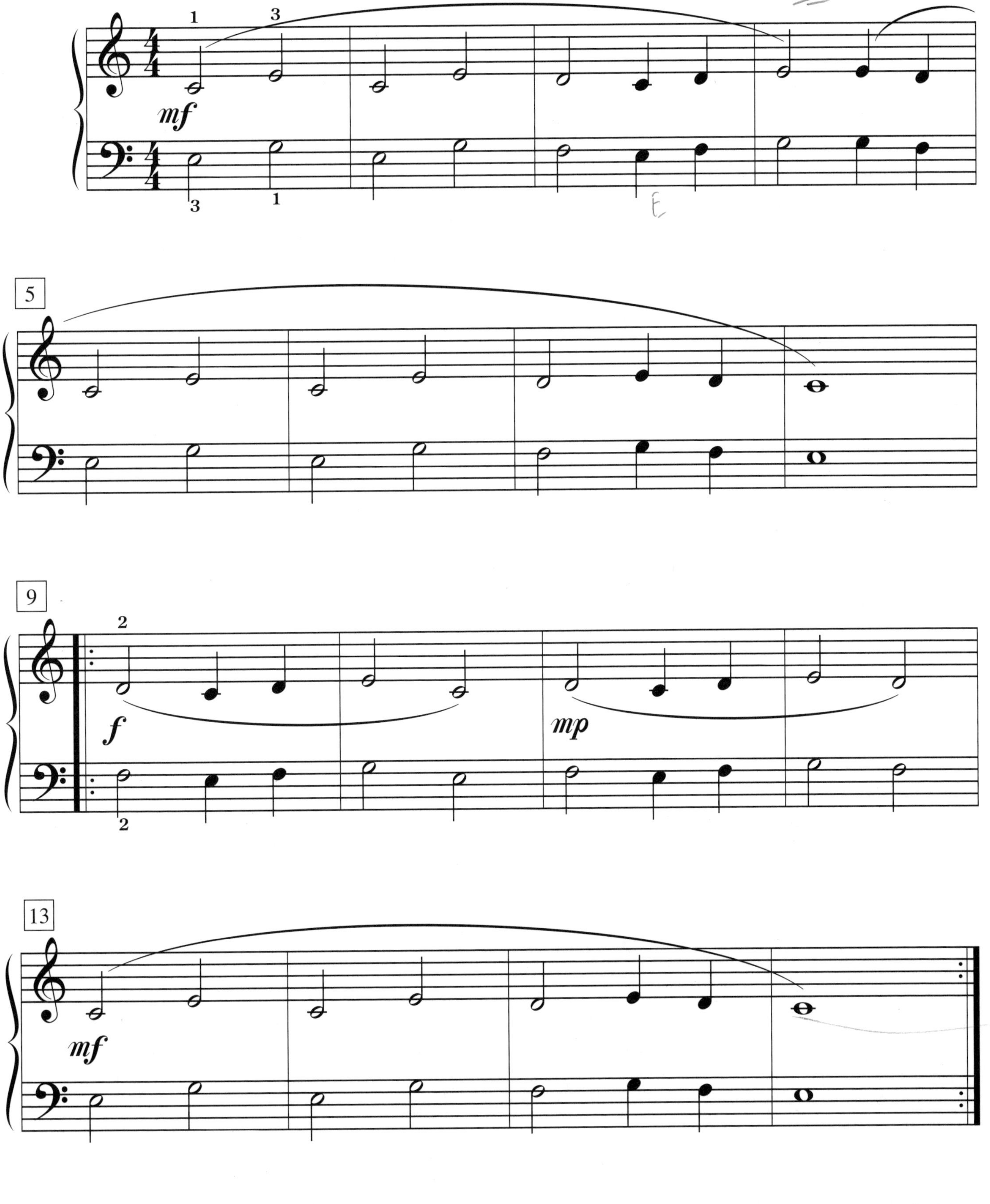

BEFORE YOU PLAY

- Compare the RH interval pattern (steps and skips) in measures 1–3. Does each measure use the same or a different interval pattern?
- On the closed key cover, "play" hands together several times.

AS YOU PLAY

Bring out the RH melody.
Do all the notes sound even?

TRANSPOSE

- *Bike Ride* is written in C major.
- Transpose to C minor. Remember the E♭.

CREATE

Vary the LH rhythm.

Example:

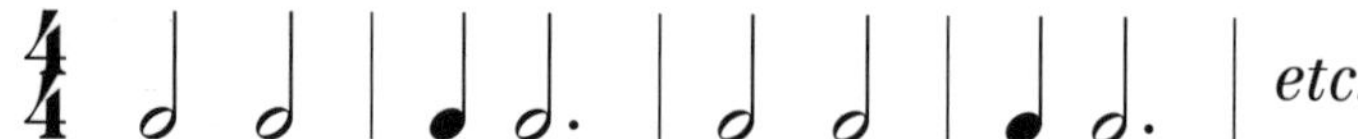

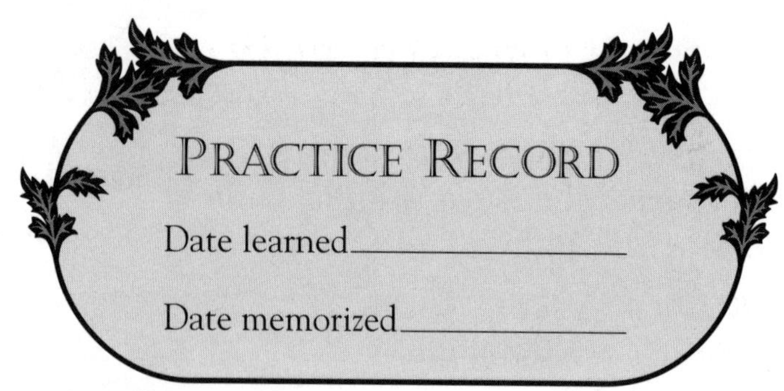

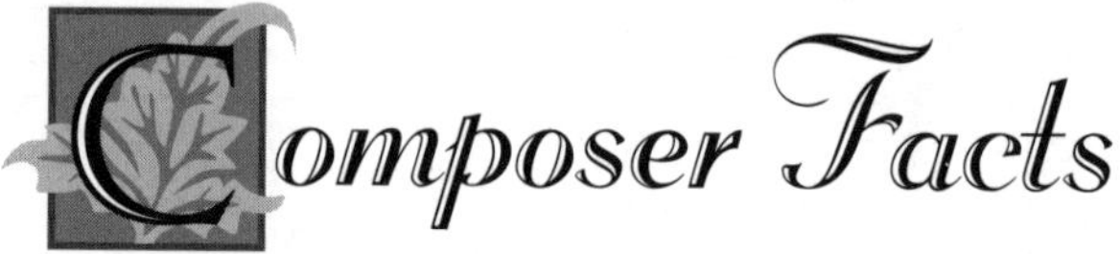

PRACTICE RECORD

Date learned__________

Date memorized__________

Composer Facts

Cornelius Gurlitt (1820–1901), German, was an organist, teacher and student of the composer, Carl Reinecke (1824–1910). Best known as a composer, Gurlitt authored over 250 works, many of which continue to be played today.

Bike Ride

Op. 82, No. 10

Cornelius Gurlitt

Moderato

Both hands one octave higher than written throughout

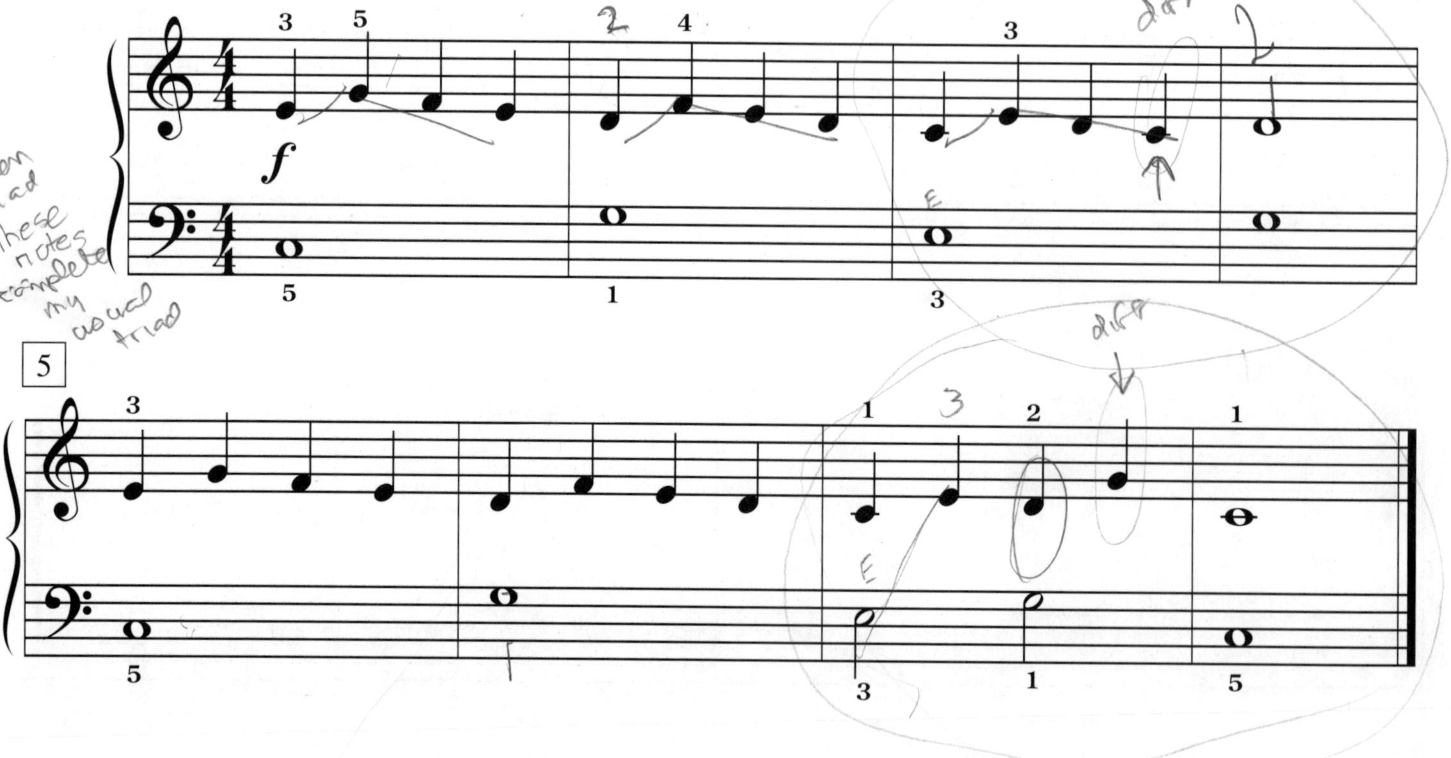

BEFORE YOU PLAY

- Compare the LH interval pattern (steps and skips) in measures 1–3. Does each measure use the same or a different interval pattern?
- On the closed key cover, "play" hands together several times.

AS YOU PLAY

Bring out the LH melody.
Do all the notes sound even?

TRANSPOSE

- *Skate Board* is written in C major.
- Transpose to C minor.
  Which note is flat? _____

CREATE

Let the RH double the LH melody. (Both hands will play the same notes at the same time, one octave apart.)

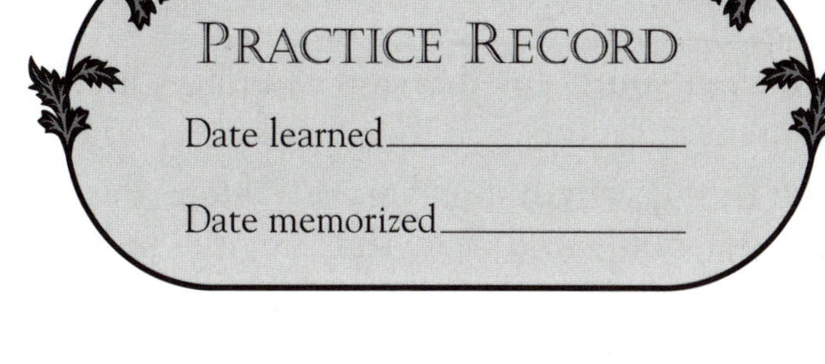

Cornelius Gurlitt (1820–1901), *see page 10.*

Skate Board

Op. 82, No. 11

Cornelius Gurlitt

Moderato

Both hands one octave higher than written throughout

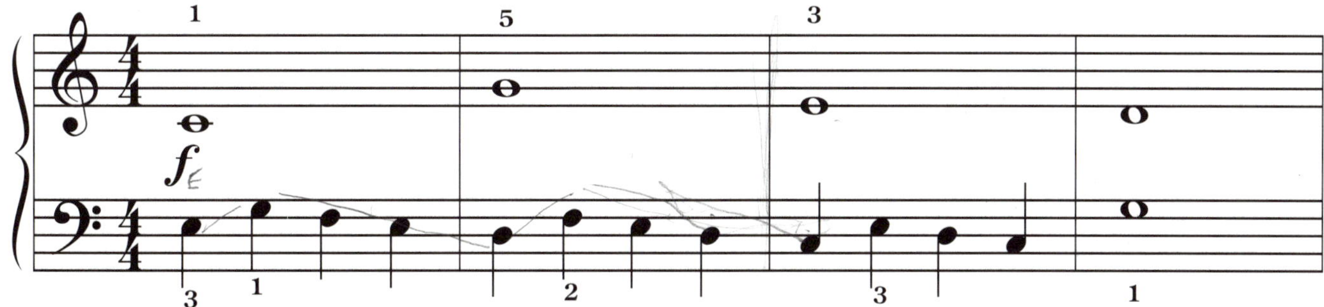

BEFORE YOU PLAY

- On the closed key cover, "play" the RH part several times. Be careful to make a different sound for the staccato notes and the slurred notes.
- Tap the RH rhythm as you say "step" for quarter notes and "trot-ting" for the pairs of eighth notes.

AS YOU PLAY

- Listen so that your playing is light and elegant.
- Be careful to not collapse your RH fifth finger in measures 1, 5 and 13.

TRANSPOSE

- *English Minuet* is written in G major. However, no F♯ is used in this piece.
- Transpose to F major.
  Which note is flat?_____

CREATE

Vary the RH rhythm in measures 1–3 and measures 5–7 by adding eighth notes.

Example:

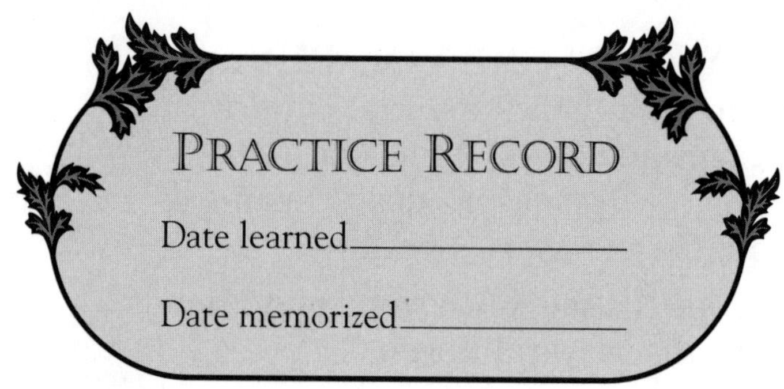

Alexander Reinagle (1756–1809), English-American, was a composer, teacher and pianist who took pride in composing for his students. In 1786, he settled in America where some historians believe he taught Nellie Custis, George Washington's daughter.

English Minuet

Alexander Reinagle

BEFORE YOU PLAY

- On the closed key cover, "play" the RH part alone. Let your wrist lift slightly ("breathe") for the rests (measures 4, 8, etc.).
- "Play" the LH alone. Do not bounce your arm when the thumb plays.

AS YOU PLAY

Listen so the RH sings over the LH accompaniment.

TRANSPOSE

- *Fairy Tale Waltz* is written in C major.
- Transpose to G major.

CREATE

- Play, starting in different octaves on the piano.
- Give the piece a new title when it is played low on the piano:

____

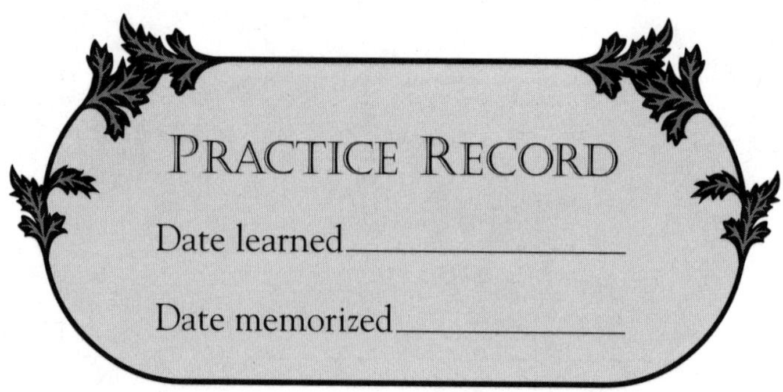

Cornelius Gurlitt (1820–1901), *see page 10.*

Fairy Tale Waltz

Op. 82, No. 18

Moderato

Cornelius Gurlitt

Both hands one octave higher than written throughout

BEFORE YOU PLAY

- On the closed key cover, slowly "play" the entire piece, hands together.
- Decide where each hand plays the melody.

AS YOU PLAY

- Listen and bring out the melody.
- Play the eighth-note rhythms precisely, like a march.

TRANSPOSE

- The RH of *Bold Knight* is written in C major.
- Transpose the RH to F major. What is the RH starting note?_____

CREATE

Make up a story about the *Bold Knight*. Include as much detail as you can.

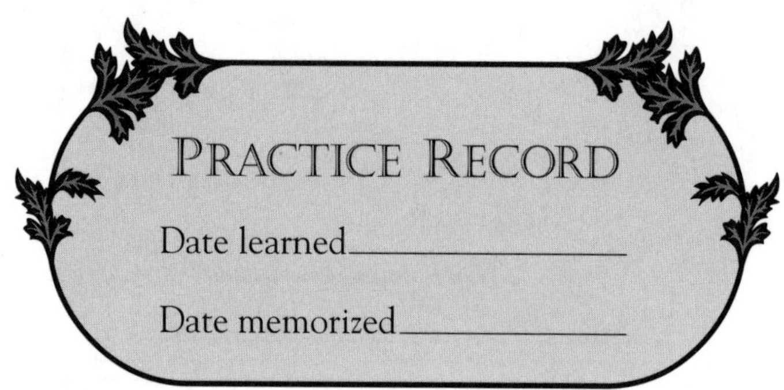

Wilhelm Moritz Vogel (1846–1922), German, was a composer, organist, teacher of piano and voice, and a music critic. He wrote choral and organ works as well as many instructional piano pieces, including a 12-volume piano method.

Bold Knight

Wilhelm Moritz Vogel

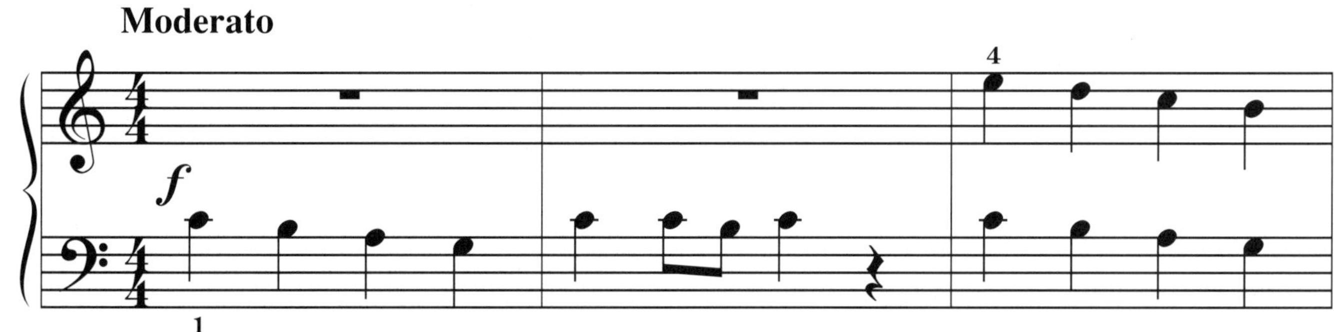

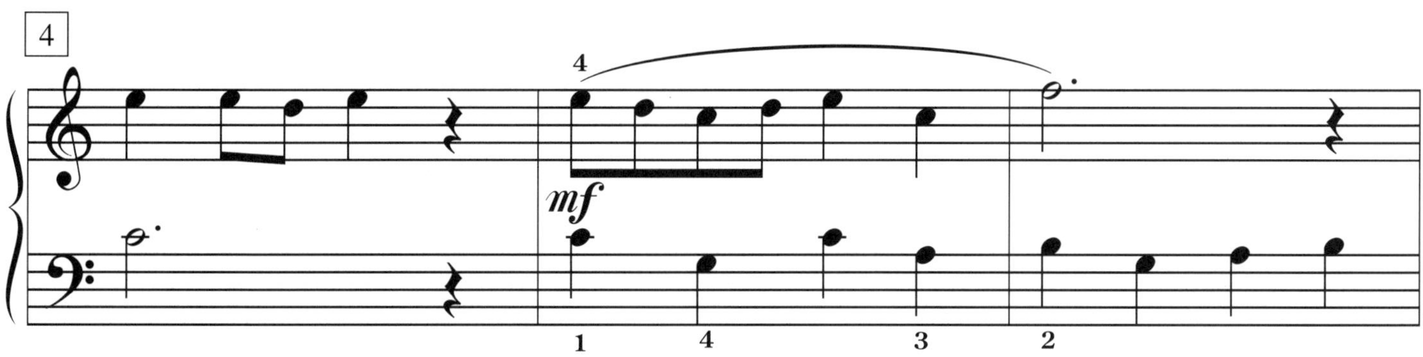

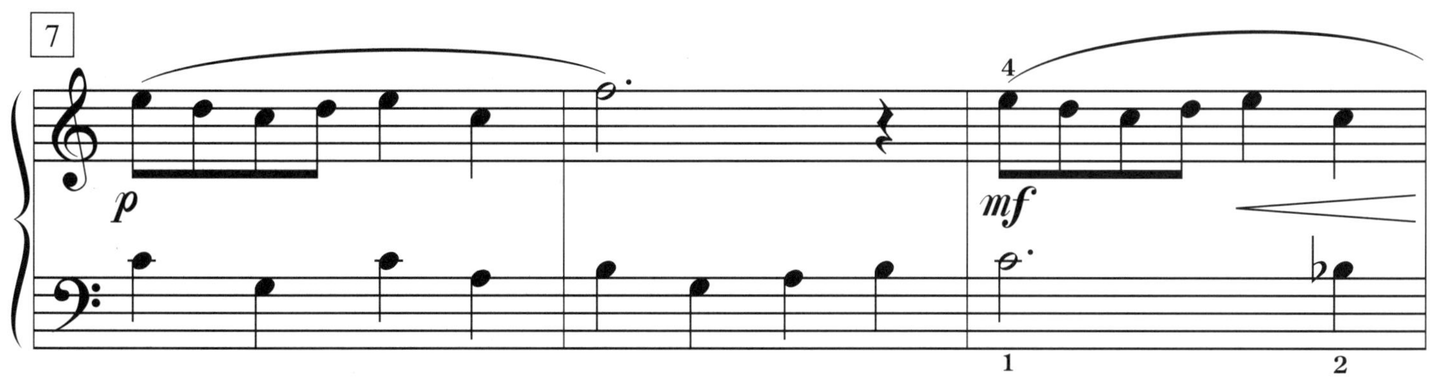

BEFORE YOU PLAY

- Tap the RH rhythm as you say "step" for quarter notes and "trot-ting" for the pairs of eighth notes.

- Decide (with your teacher) if you will play the optional LH notes. On the piano keyboard, practice the LH alone for measures 1–8.

AS YOU PLAY

- The RH repeated notes should sound like gentle laughing.
- Listen carefully so that all the LH chord tones sound exactly together.

TRANSPOSE

- *Laughing* is written in C major.
- Transpose to D major.

CREATE

Vary the LH part by playing broken chords.

Example:

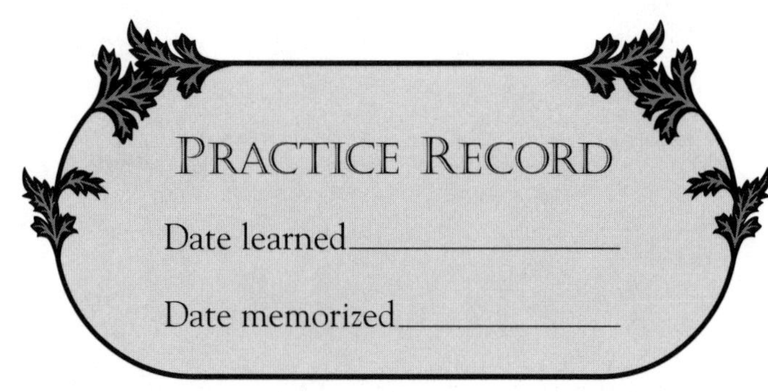

Carl Czerny (1791–1857), Austrian, was a composer, a student of Beethoven (1770–1827) and the teacher of Franz Liszt (1811–1886). He was a famous virtuoso pianist who is best remembered for his thousands of exercises for piano.

NOTE TO TEACHER: Czerny originally notated this piece in $\frac{2}{4}$ time using sixteenth, eighth and half notes.

Laughing

Op. 777, No. 2

Carl Czerny

Allegro

Both hands one octave higher than written throughout

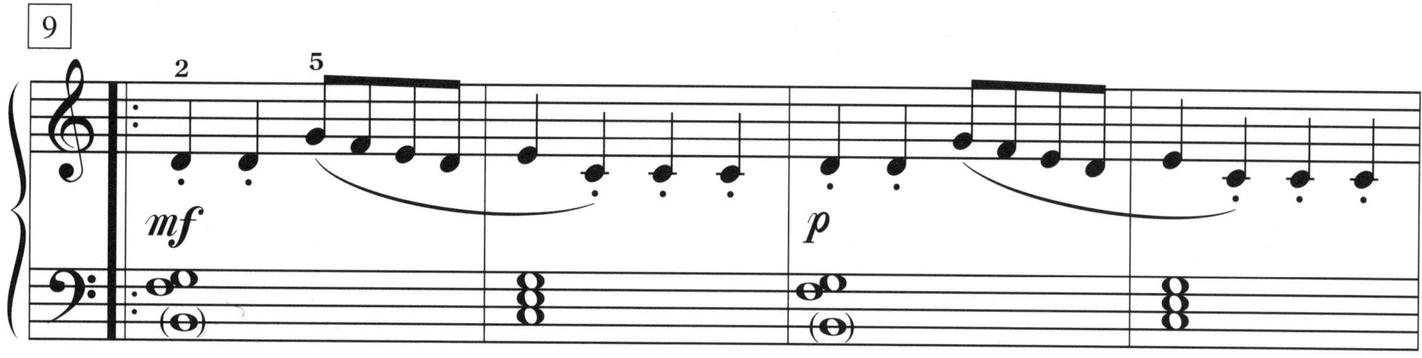

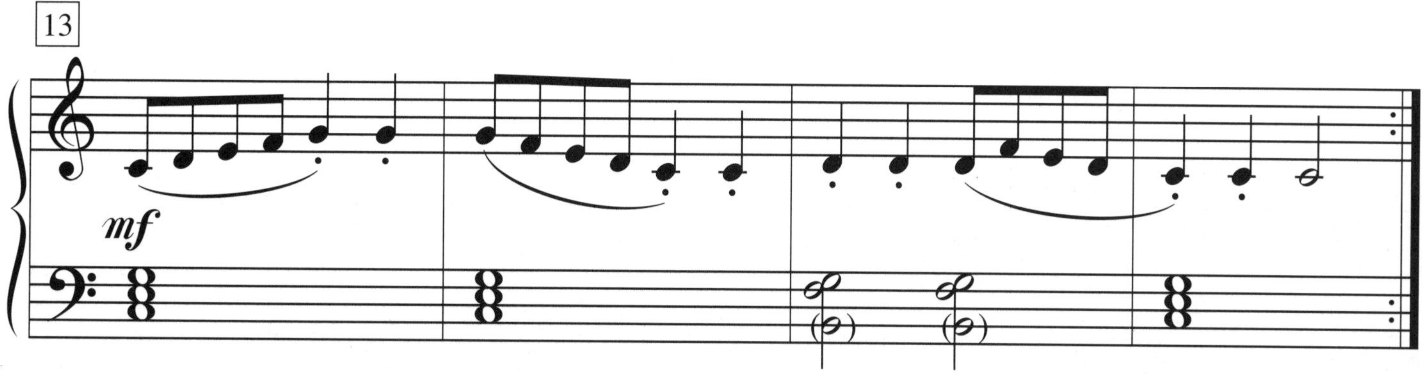

* Notes in parentheses are optional for small hands.
Eliminating these notes will maintain the five-finger pattern.

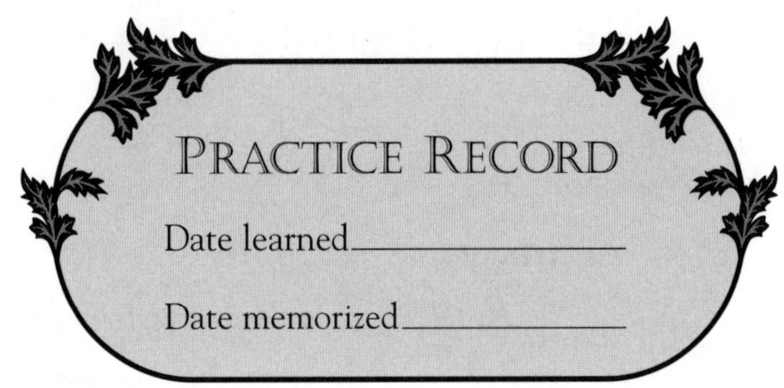

BEFORE YOU PLAY

On the closed key cover, "play" the two-note slurs, hands separately. Use small "down-up" motions of the hand and wrist, like graceful bowing.

AS YOU PLAY

Listen carefully so that the second note of each slur is not too short and "brittle."

TRANSPOSE

- *Promenade* is written in D major. However, no C♯ is used in the piece.
- Transpose to D minor. What note is different in D minor?____

CREATE

- Add words to the RH of measures 1–4.
- What mood do you wish to create with your words?

____

Elena Gnessina (1874– ?), Russian, was an outstanding concert pianist and educator. She and her sisters founded one of the most famous music conservatories in Moscow, the Gnessin Institute.

Promenade

Elena Gnessina

Andante grazioso

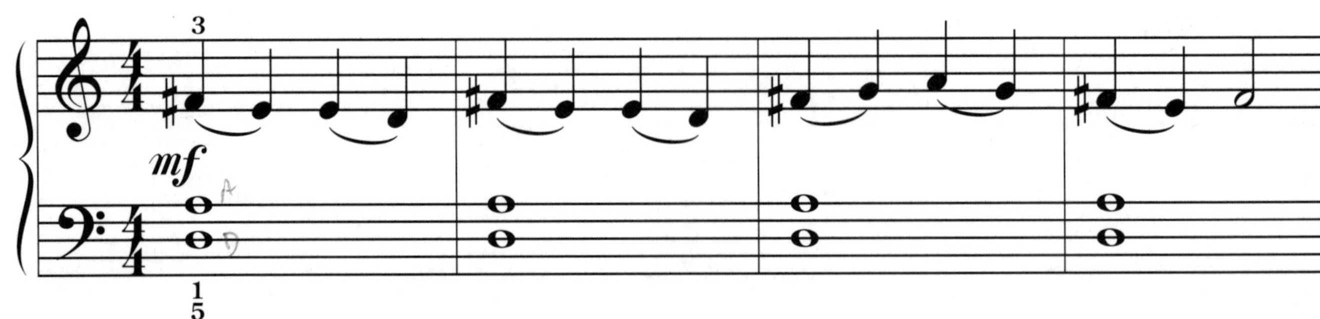

BEFORE YOU PLAY
On the closed key cover, practice hands separately. Let the wrists gently rise through the three-note slurs.

AS YOU PLAY
Listen for gentle endings for each slur.

TRANSPOSE
- *My Shadow is* written in G major. However, no F# is used in the piece.
- Transpose to C major. What is the starting RH note?____

CREATE
Play the LH louder than the RH.

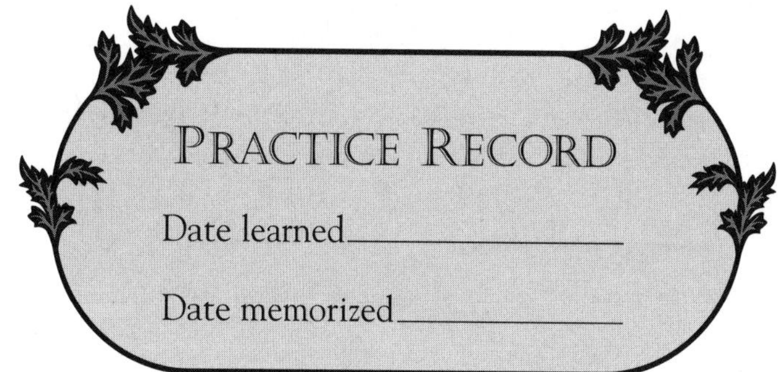

(Christian) Louis (Heinrich) Köhler (1820–1886), German, was a conductor, teacher and critic, as well as composer of over 300 works, most of which were piano etudes written for his own students.

My Shadow

Op. 218, No. 18

Louis Köhler

Allegretto

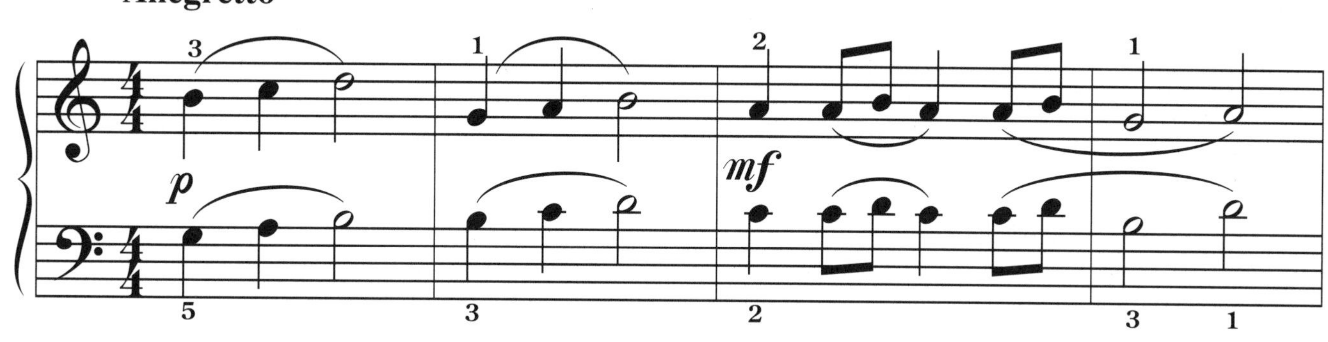

BEFORE YOU PLAY

Notice how Bartók wrote the LH rhythm in measure 7. Another way to write it would be:

"trot-ting trot-ting step trot-ting"

AS YOU PLAY

Listen for the graceful rise and fall of the melody. The changing lengths of the slurs help make this piece sound interesting.

TRANSPOSE

- *Song of Spring* is written in G major. However, no F♯ is used in the piece.
- Transpose to D major.

CREATE

- Write your own dynamics for this piece.
- What mood do you create with your changes?

____

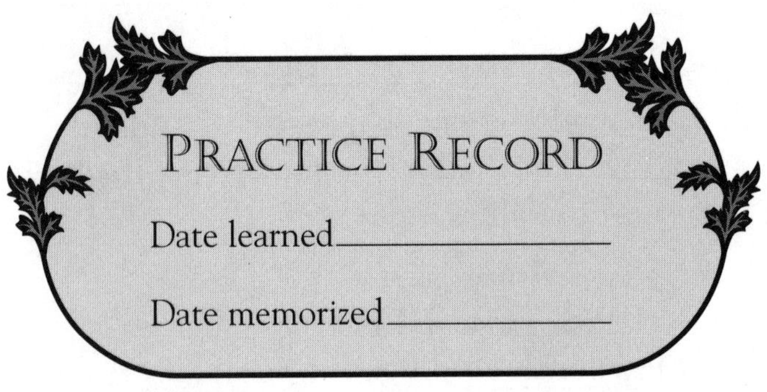

Béla Bartók (1881–1945), Hungarian, was a composer, pianist and ethnomusicologist (one who studies the cultural sources of music). Sometimes his compositions used ancient scales (called modes), and he often ignored the rules of traditional harmony.

Song of Spring

(from First Term at the Piano)

Béla Bartók

Moderato

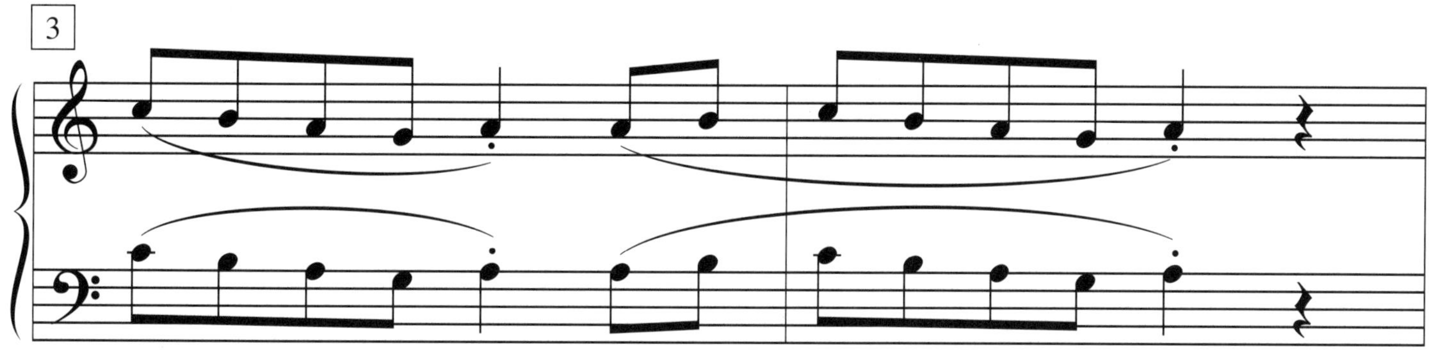

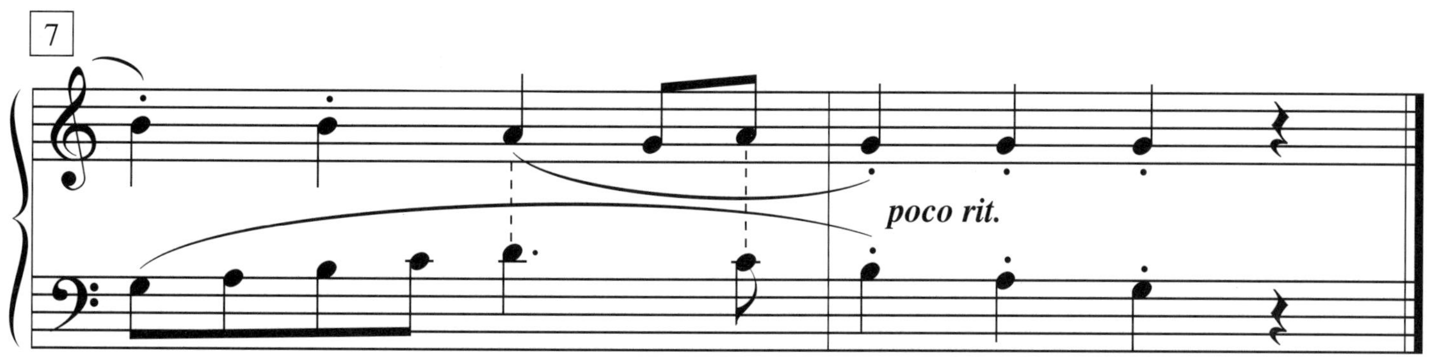

BEFORE YOU PLAY

- Tap the rhythm, hands together on your lap.
- On the closed key cover, "play" the RH alone, being careful of the slurs and staccatos.

AS YOU PLAY

- Listen for sudden dynamic changes at measures 11 and 13.
- Play the staccato notes with a light thumb. Do not bounce your arm.

TRANSPOSE

- *At the Playground* is written in F major.
- Transpose to C major.

CREATE

Vary the RH rhythm by playing a "long-short" pattern for every two eighth notes.

Example:

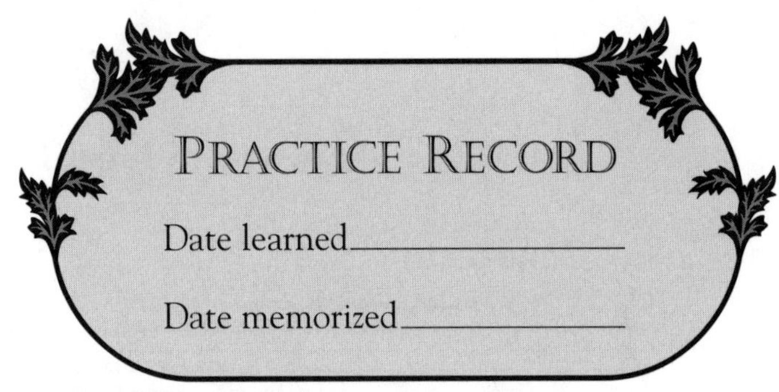

Heinrich Wohlfahrt (1797–1883), German, was a piano teacher, writer and composer who lived in Leipzig, Germany. He is best known for his piano music for students.

At the Playground

(from Musical ABC)

Heinrich Wohlfahrt

BEFORE YOU PLAY

On the closed key cover, "play" measures 9–12, hands together several times.

AS YOU PLAY

- Listen for a graceful phrase "shape" in measures 1–4, measures 5–8 and measures 13–16.
- Notice the sudden dynamic changes at measures 9 and 11.

TRANSPOSE

- *Little Romance* is written in D minor. However, no B♭ is used in the piece.
- Transpose to A minor and D major.

CREATE

Change the rhythm in each measure so that the time signature is $\frac{4}{4}$, not $\frac{3}{4}$.

Example:

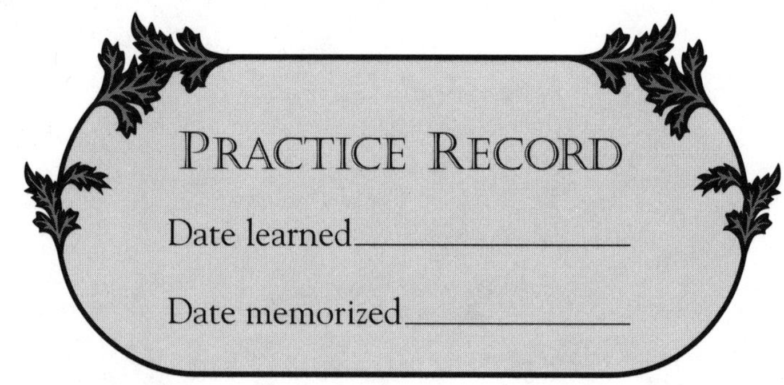

Heinrich Wohlfahrt (1797–1883), *see page 24.*

Little Romance

(from Musical ABC)

Heinrich Wohlfahrt

BEFORE YOU PLAY

- There are two RH melodic patterns that use eighth notes. Which one occurs most often? Compare the two patterns to see how they are different. In measure 12, which melodic pattern is transposed?
- On the closed key cover, "play" hands together several times.

AS YOU PLAY

- Listen for a strong RH melody, with a gentle LH part in the background.
- Play firm, insistent tenutos in measures 9–10 and measures 13–14.

TRANSPOSE

- *Folk Dance* is written in F major.
- Transpose measures 1–8 to A major and to A minor.

CREATE

- Play *Folk Dance* at a much slower tempo.
- Give the piece a new title to fit the mood of the slower tempo:

____

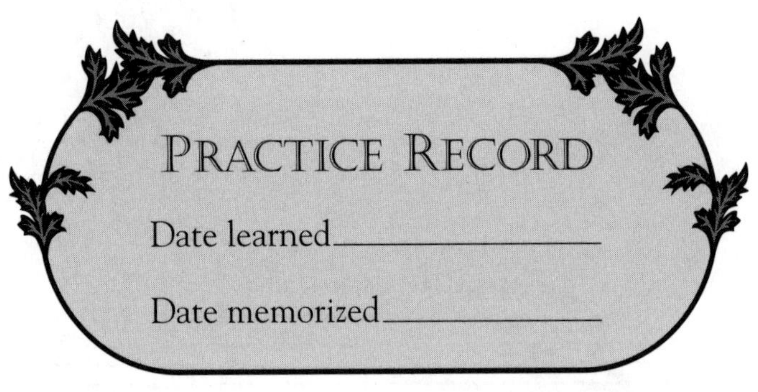

Heinrich Wohlfahrt (1797–1883), *see page 24.*

Folk Dance

(from Musical ABC)

Allegro Heinrich Wohlfahrt

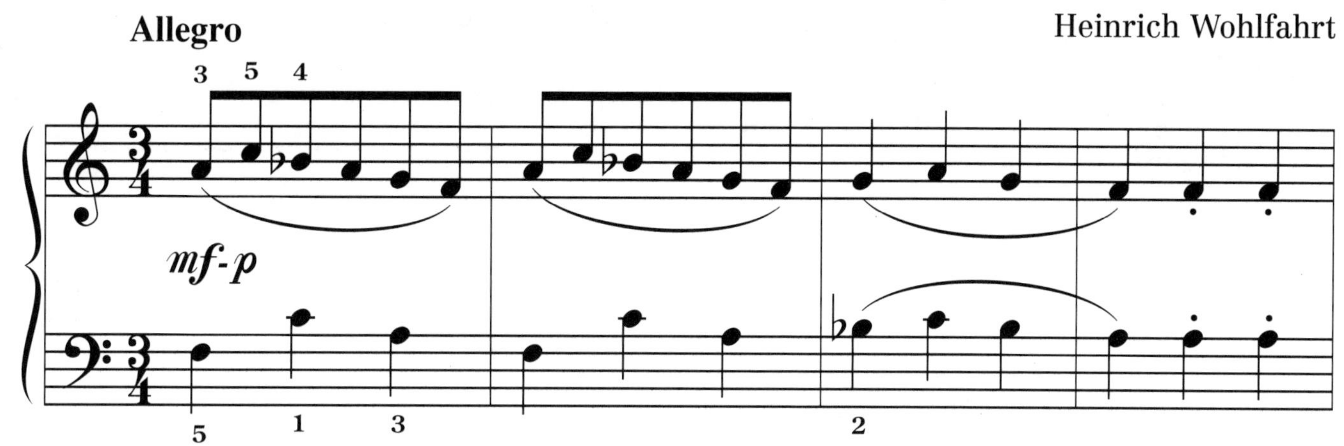

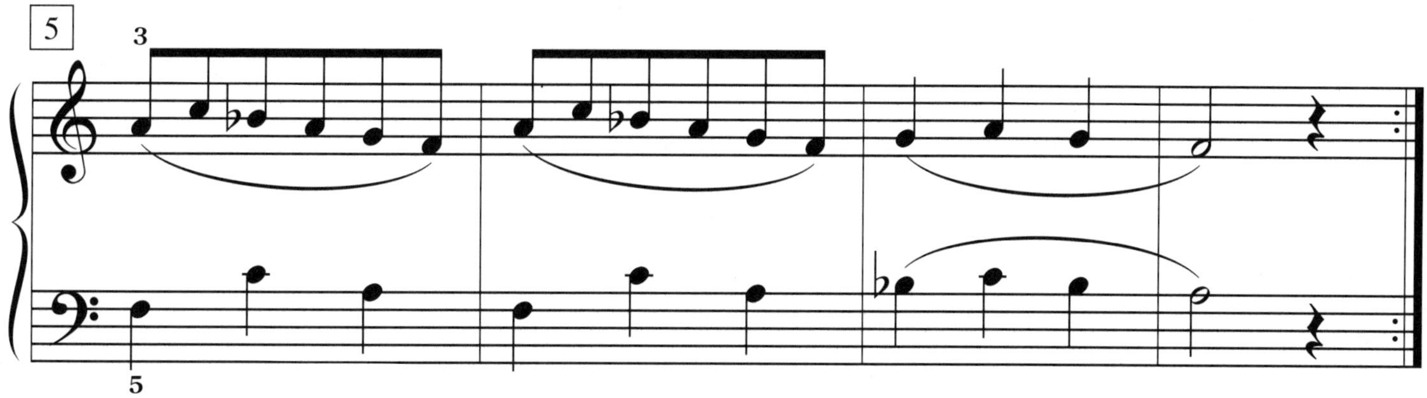

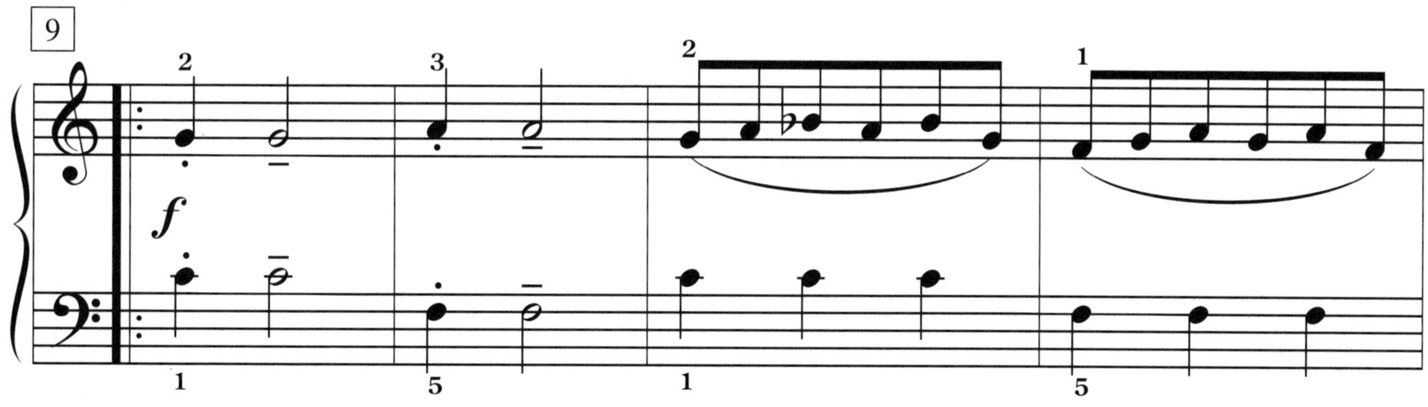

BEFORE YOU PLAY

- On the piano keyboard, silently place both hands in position for measures 1 and 2, then for measures 9 and 10. (Each hand position change is indicated by a circled finger number.)
- On the closed key cover, tap the rhythm, hands together.
  Say:

Find the two measures where this rhythm does not occur in either hand.

AS YOU PLAY

- Listen for both parts of the conversation. Do both hands contribute equally? Does one hand play louder than the other?
- Notice the LH part is written in the treble clef beginning in measure 10.

TRANSPOSE

- *Conversation* is written in A minor.
- Transpose measures 1–8 to D minor and A major.

CREATE

- Play in different octaves on the piano (very high, then very low) for a different mood.
- What might each conversation (in the different octaves) be about?

____

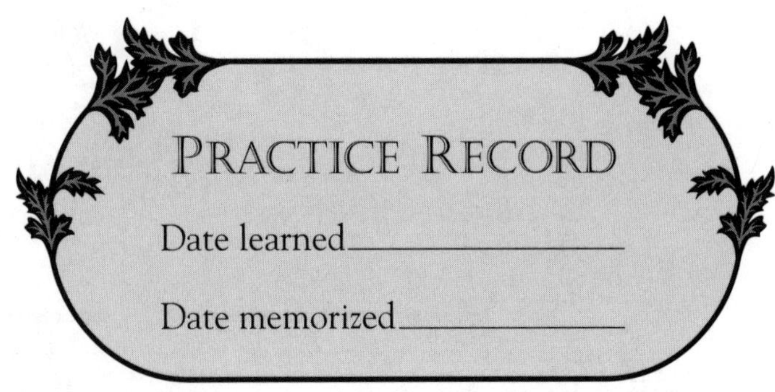

Ferdinand Beyer (1803–1863), *see page 4.*

Conversation

Op. 101, No. 60

Ferdinand Beyer

Glossary

TEMPO

allegro	fast and lively
allegretto	a little fast and lively; a little slower than ***allegro***
moderato	moderate (medium) tempo
andante	walking tempo
ritardando (rit.)	a gradual slowing of the tempo

DYNAMICS (from loudest to softest)

forte (f)	loud
mezzo forte (mf)	moderately (medium) loud
mezzo piano (mp)	moderately (medium) soft
piano (p)	soft
accent (>)	play this note louder than those around it
crescendo (cresc.)	gradually becoming louder
diminuendo (dim.)	gradually becoming softer

ARTICULATIONS

slur (‿)	a curved line over or under notes that means to play ***legato***
staccato **(·)**	to play detached (not ***legato***); disconnected
tenuto **(–)**	hold the note(s) the full length; slight stress

OTHER

con moto	with motion
da capo al fine (D. C. al Fine)	go back to the beginning and repeat again until ***Fine***
etude	a study; a piece that has a technical purpose
Fine	the end
flat	lower the note a half step
grazioso	gracefully
minuet	a graceful dance, alway in $\frac{3}{4}$ time
poco	a little
promenade	a piece for "strolling about"
repeat	to play again
scherzando	playful
sharp	raise the note a half step
transpose	to play in a different key (pattern). The intervals remain the same, but the actual notes change.
whole-tone scale	a scale of all whole steps, six in an octave